MW01225265

leave me

the fuck

alone

leave me

the fuck

alone

jamie s.

leave me the fuck alone

this is a

message for you.

leave me

the fuck

alone

you need to

seriously

leave me

the fuck alone.

i honestly
don't understand
why you keep
trying to contact me.

please,

stop.

you may believe
that i'm not
being truthful,
but i really am.

i've never
been so honest
before in my
entire life.

back off!

when i wake up
in the morning,
i don't want
a headache
just because i know
you'll contact me
yet again.

i'm fabulous,
but you just need
to stop calling me.

don't send me
any emails either.

that would
piss me off more
because i hardly
check that account,
and i don't want to
see your name when i do.

i thought you would
understand
that this also meant
for you to not send me
any text messages.

i'm too cheap
to pay for that feature,
and your messages of
the word
hello
are costing me
20cents,
three times per day.

just stop.

this is getting embarrassing
for both of us.

for you,
because you seem
like a creeper.

for me,
because i now
feel some second-hand
embarrassment for you.

ugh,

excuse me …

…

do not contact

my brother.

he don't know

who you are.

did you just

post a photo of me

on your social media page?

like the profile photo?

you best remove

that shit

REAL

quick.

i can't deal
with stupid
anymore.

i just can't.

i owe you nothing.

so why you keep
hounding me down
like the collection's agency?

people tell me
to block your number,
but it seems
my phone don't have
that option.

crap ...

why you leaving
me a message
on my voicemail?

i only have space for
three voice messages.

i need those spaces free
for someone i actually
want to hear from.

you haven't found
someone else to
bother yet?

go get a dog.

don't ask sophia

about me.

the girl don't like you.

don't drive around
my neighborhood
then call me
saying that you're
going up and down the streets,
seeing if i'm outside.

it's the middle of
january.

why would i
be walking up and down
the streets,
fool?

that best not be you

ringing my doorbell

at 3PM in the

afternoon.

you don't have
a job to go to?!

you all sorts of

creepy.

zane just cheated on
marie with alexander,
who is married to hunter,
who is secretly
having a baby with anna-boujie.

i'm trying to watch
my soaps.

stop bothering me.

oh …

you brought me
a flower …

how funny.
i think my neighbor
has a bunch of those
growing in her
front lawn …

no, you

CANNOT

come in.

go back to work.

shit.

you plan
on deleting that
photo of me
off social media,
right?

did anna-boujie

just confess that

the baby ain't hunter's?

i missed

some juicy parts

in my soap.

it was great

seeing you.

why this fool

texting me

still?

i don't want a
photo.

stop sending me
this garbage,
or i'll change
my number.

. . .

get both you
AND the collection's agency
off my ass.

are you talking

to my neighbor?

GO HOME!

shit.

i'm not desperate.

i'm not pathetic.

i don't need you.

every time you come around,
i get the runs afterwards.

clearly my body is
trying to rid some toxins.

you're not hot

enough

to be this much

of a crazy.

stop it

right now.

repeat after me:

it's time to

move on.

fool,

is that you

hiding near the bush

in my backyard?

i can see you
behind the bush.

it's the middle of
winter.

you're wearing black
when there's white snow
everywhere.

idiot.

this is ridiculous.

if you wanted me
so badly,
you shouldn't have
done me wrong
and pissed me off.

don't call me
pretending to be emotional,
pretending to cry.

you're too old and ugly
to pull off a cute pout.

the shit coming out

your mouth

is worse than

what comes out

your ass every morning.

don't send your mail

to my house so you

have an excuse to come here.

<u>RETURN TO SENDER</u>

if you put as much
time towards bettering yourself
as you do towards
bothering the hell out of me,
maybe you could keep
a partner without lies,
tricks, and manipulation.

wah dat?

that a
DICK PIC?

the hell made
you think i'd want
to see that thing?

dude,

you have some

serious

problems.

if you don't have
anything better to do,
go read a book.

let me hand
you one.

you need to

seriously

just leave me

the fuck alone.

jamie s.

Manufactured by Amazon.ca
Bolton, ON

17171518R00033